My Financial Journey

What NOT to Do with Money

By Sheri Simmons

This is a work of fiction. All the characters, events, incidents, names, organizations and places portrayed in this novel are either products of the author's imagination or are used fictitiously. Any resemblance to actual persons, living or dead, business establishments, events or locales is entirely coincidental.

ISBN: 978-0-9853199-5-3

Acknowledgments

I have been a published author for six years and I am truly blessed to share book number six with you. This has been a truly awesome journey. I have met many great people in the past six years. Yara Kaleemah, thank you for being my friend for all these years. It has been such a pleasure working with you on projects. You are truly a caring, genuine individual.

During my six year journey as an author I stumbled upon the financial industry. Who would have thought that I would be in the finance industry? Definitely not me!!! The past nine months have been amazing. I have learned and grown personally and career wise. I always thought I would be just an author. Now I found something else that I love to do and talk about. Through this business, I have met so many people from all over the US and Canada. There are so many people I want to thank, so if your name is not here, blame it on my mind and not my heart.

Thank you Jonathan Mehrian for your powerful leadership. I appreciate the opportunity to personally learn from you. I look forward to doing big things with you.

To the West Los Angeles team, even though we are on different coast, I want to learn from you all. I had a blast in San Jose and want to come to LA to get some training. We rock as the #1 baseshop!!! #TeamTamashi

Thank you to Aaron Pagan for being a person of true integrity, and good character. Not too many people in the world are like you. I am glad to know that you are my friend and have my back. Thank you for helping and teaching me to be great. Thank you for reminding me to stay true to myself and not have anyone change me. You don't know how much your presence means to me.

Michelle Maloloyon, thanks for your relentless leadership. You are the true definition of what a Boss

Thank you to all my readers and supporters over the years, thank you, thank, thank you. I wouldn't be here with book number six today. I see all your reviews and cannot express how much it all means to me.

About the Author

Sheri Simmons is a Jill of all trades. She loves to use her passions to help others with their dreams and goals. She is an author of five books and currently working on two (including her memoir). She is a part of a National Financial Literacy Campaign. She works hand and hand with families to help them get their personal finances in order. In addition to helping people personally, she also serves as a speaker with the organization RAINN (Rape, Abuse, Incest National Network). Through this organization, she has attended several events speaking out against domestic violence and sexual assault. Her passion to help people runs very deep and she has plans to continue to help wherever she sees fit.

Sheri is a licensed Financial Educator. She holds licenses in multiple states. The services she provides are very diversified. She can assist with retirement planning, estate planning, college planning. (She is a Certified College Coach), life insurance, long term care and medicare supplements. She can be reached at (201)565-2796 or SheriSimmons.WSB@gmail.com.

Introduction

No one taught me about money. I knew money was a need for anything that I wanted in life. I grew up in New York City. I was born and raised in the Bronx until age seven. Then my family moved to East Harlem. It was there, that I spent the next seven years of my life watching people live lives that weren't their reality. People walking around in the latest fashion, but a day away from eviction. People driving fancy cars but couldn't afford the car note. Now that I think back to my childhood, I see that I learned very bad habits. How to get money but not keep it. How to just spend and not save. How to get into debt and

cruel place without the guidance of parents and other trustworthy adults. I had no idea what I was going to do with my new independent life. It took sixteen years for me to discover that everything I was doing financially was wrong.

I attended Hunter college my freshman year. I was majoring in elementary education. When I first selected, the major I was content. But as time went on I became uninterested in teaching. My first job as a student was in the senior center as at Hunter College. It was a work study position. There was no set wage. My pay was based on the amount of federal money that was provided to work study students. I was happy to be working and making money. It wasn't much but it was my first job. In addition to the money I made from work study, I also received a financial aid refund. Of course, at eighteen, I knew nothing about saving. So, I spent every single penny on clothes, clubs, and miscellaneous things. I didn't have any responsibility at eighteen. I had left my mother's house and was staying with a friend. So, I didn't have any bills except for a cellphone. All I knew was spend, spend, spend. If I was financially literate I would have been saving for my retirement. At eighteen, I don't think anyone is thinking about their retirement. I know I wasn't. Now I'm thirty five with a ten year retirement plan. If I had started back then I could have retired now.

Retirement isn't about age. The average person will say that they want to retire at sixty five. Why? Retirement has to do with having money to live comfortably without working. So we don't have to wait till sixty five. However the average person has an employee mindset. They work 40 hours for 40 years and then retire off of 40% of what they earned. Retirement needs to be planned out. If it isn't there will be lots of people in their sixty's and seventy heading back to the workforce. People have 401k's and pension plans but don't know how they work. They just sign up for their employer benefits because someone else said. If people understood how money works and the different types of accounts and tax advantages they wouldn't be so quick to put their money in tax deferred account. If only people had access to all the financial information that one percent know. What if I told you that the information is available. But it doesn't matter if none of what you learn is applied. I am here to tell you today that knowledge isn't power. Applied Knowledge is power. We could learn everything we want in the world but with no application we wasted our time gathering information. What's the point of gathering information if we aren't going to use it. I hope that if you picked this book up that you plan to use it in one way shape or form (Not as a coaster or doorstop lol) I have included lined pages for you to take notes. If you have any questions feel free to contact me. This book is not meant to answer all of your financial questions. I am not a lawyer, accountant or investor (working on it). This book is meant to introduce financial concepts and get you to think about your financial situation in new light. Hopefully this book is the change that you need to make. Being financially illiterate is nothing to be ashamed of. I was for a long time. Once we admit to ourselves that we need to change. We must decide to change our financial future. If you are ready to do so continue reading. If not, it's perfectly fine. When you are the information will still be here.

Saving (How to save and where to save)

When you think of saving money, where is the first place you think to do so? If you said the bank, that is correct. However, there is a problem with saving money in a bank. The interest rates are ridiculously low. Your money isn't going to grow in a bank. In fact, the bank gives us 0.14% (more or less) in interest and then turns around and lend us money with 15-20% interest rates. Don't believe me, check out your bank statement for your interest rate. Check how much interest you earned on your statement. Is that doing anything to grow the money that you are saving??

There is a rule that we must know and remember when it comes to money. It's known as the rule of 72. Simply put it tells us how quickly our money will double by dividing the interest rate by 72. Now take your bank interest rate and divide it by 72. What did you get? Are you satisfied with the number of years it will take your money to grow? I know I am not and I have re-positioned my money to saving vehicles that will grow my money. Growing money is how people become rich and wealthy. They make the money work for them.

Deciding where to put your money for growth is not going to be an easy decision.When I discovered this information. It was a no brainer to me. I wanted my money to grow. So many factors to think about. I can tell you that where ever you save your money should be in a tax advantaged account. It should also have an interest rate of 6% or more to beat inflation and taxes. I know all these terms are probably new or not clear. No worries, I am going to explain all these terms in full details.

What is inflation? Over the course of time our dollar value decreases. I know it still may be confusing so here's an example. When I was eight years old, I was able to go to the corner store (I'm from New York City) and get four bags of potato chips for $1.00. Now twenty-seven years later, my eight year old can't do that. He can only get two bags or a large bag for the same dollar. The same dollar and yet it gets him less than what it got me. Another example would be buying groceries. What we used to be able to buy with $100 in the supermarket does not get us much now. I say to myself how come I spend $100 but come out with very few bags? Inflation at it's finest. We need to be mindful of inflation's existent. What we can live off of now will not be the case five to ten years from now.

Now that you know what inflation is, lets move on to a topic most people dread. Taxes! Nobody likes paying taxes. Let's face it we pay taxes for any and everything under the sun. Benjamin Franklin said that nothing is certain but death and taxes. And that is nothing but the truth. We pay taxes when we work, We pay taxes when we spend, and we pay taxes when we die. Yes when you die, your estate will be taxed if it's over a certain amount. So we must be mindful of taxes while we are trying to save, grow and protect our money.

There are many options available to keep your money in. Most people only know about Tax Now accounts. These accounts consist of checking, savings, CD's, and stocks. With these accounts, at the end of the year you will have to pay taxes on any interest earned. However, these accounts don't provide much interest. And don't be fooled by those high interest accounts. The 2-3% is not enough to beat inflation which is between 3-4%. Inflation and taxes eat up your money, preventing it from growing to its full potential. However, by placing your money in accounts with high interest you can make up for the loss of inflation and taxes.

The second types of accounts that are available to us are called tax later accounts. These would be 401ks, 403b, Ira, and Pensions. These accounts are popular with employees so they can save for their retirement. It's always a good thing to save for your retirement. The earlier the better. The issue with this account is that the money you are contributing is not being taxed at contribution. It's taxed at withdrawal. When you go to take your money, you will be taxes, but at an unknown tax rate. We only know the current tax rate. We don't know the future tax rate. Plus if you withdraw money before fifty nine and a half, your money is subjected to early withdrawal penalties. If you plan to use one of these accounts, make sure that you don't put all your money in there. Diversify the accounts where you put your money to maximize your growth potential.

The last type of accounts are known as tax advantaged. A small amount people know about these accounts. They are Roth IRA's, 529 college savings plans, life insurance and long term care. These accounts are taxed at contribution and distributed tax free. When I discovered the different types of accounts, it made sense to me to have a couple from each category. I ended up re-positioning funds from accounts I had to new accounts. I have seen a major difference in my savings. And it helps to know that when I need money I can get some of it tax free. Who doesn't like tax free money.

I bet you didn't expect life insurance to be on the list. Most people have so many misconceptions about life insurance. So did I, until I became a licensed agent. I learned so much about what life insurance is and it is not. I have a whole chapter dedicated on life insurance. Take notes and be prepared to take immediate massive action.

A 529 college plan is offered by individual states. It is a plan to save money for your children specifically for college. It's an investment account. If you invest here you run the risk of losing money and gaining money. But what happens if your child decides not to go to college? If you have more than one child you can transfer the account to another child. If you do not have another child, the account becomes subject to tax penalty if withdrawn for non college purposes. These plans are great to have if you know for a fact that your child is going to college. But do we know at a child's birth what their adult plans are? Most parents automatically assume their child wants to go to college. It's more of a demand and not a choice. College isn't for everyone. And for some of us who graduate, we don't even end up where we want to be. Decisions to open accounts should be made carefully.

A Roth IRA is similar to a IRA. The difference is how the contributions are taxed. With a Roth IRA the funds are taxed when you put them in. When you withdraw, the money is distributed tax free. Me personally, I love tax free money. Of course we have to pay taxes either way but I'll rather pay up front and get my money without worrying about Uncle Sam.

Out of all these accounts which ones do you have?

____

____

____

____

Which ones have you not heard of?

____

____

____

____

Which ones are you interested in learning more about?

Each of these accounts serve individual purposes. What is a good fit for one family may not be a good fit for another. For me I wouldn't be comfortable with a 401k. The one thing that I do know about money is that I don't want to lose it. And that's the risk of having a 401k. Along with fees to have someone manage the account. Don't believe me, ask anyone who lost money in 2008-2009 when the stock market crashed. I have a friend who lost $19,000 from her 401k. $19,000 is a lot of money to lose especially if you are close to retiring. And to think that this happened at a blink of an eye. No one was warned of this devastating event. If they were I'm sure most would have re-positioned their money.

Now that you have knowledge of different accounts are you going to do anything different with your saving? I know after learning this exact information I immediately started investing my money into tax advantaged accounts. Knowledge is power but applied knowledge is the true power. If you still need assistance figuring out which account is best for you that's perfectly fine. Financial literacy can be scary and overwhelming. But knowing more about your money will prepare you and your family for the long run.

One service that I provide is a financial analysis. I sit with a family one and one, and take a look at their monthly expenses and income. Most people say that they are broke and can't save anything. Sometimes it's not true. After taking a closer look, they have a lot of money slipping through the cracks. Money that at the end they can't account for. So through the analysis I can point out things that people aren't aware of that are bad habits. Eating out is great. I do it but I learned to do it in moderation. Getting the latest cell phone or car is great if you want to retire broke, or not have money to send your kids to college.I used to be that person getting the latest phone, buying things I didn't need. All of those things weren't helping me in the long run. It's never to late to get on financial track. But you have to decide to start. It's one thing to say you are going to do something. It's another to decide to do it. If you need help feel free to reach out to me and I'll be glad to help you.

Retirement Saving

What does retirement have to do with? Age or Money?The correct answer is money. If you ask ten people what age they want to retire eight most likely will say 65. The other two may be bold and say between 40 and 60. You do not have to wait till you're 65 to retire. If you have enough money to retire comfortably at 30 then feel free to retire. But do you know how much you need to retire?

Most people contribute to their employers retirement benefit plans. These are 401k's, 457 and 403B. They are pretty much the same thing. The numbers indicate who you work for. A private company, government or non profit organization. The issue with these accounts is that people get them but don't understand how they work. They have money deducted from their paychecks and have no idea what is going on with their money. We need to be our own money managers. We shouldn't be placing our money in an account and not know what's going on with it. Then there's the issue of taxes. When you put money in a 401k you are not taxed. You become taxed when you go to withdraw the money. Withdrawing the money before 59 1/2 has a tax penalty. And you must withdraw your funds before 70 1/2 or pay a penalty. We only know the current tax rate. Who knows what the tax rate will be in the future? So you are leaving your money somewhere not knowing what you have to pay in taxes. Personally I wouldn't do it but this is my opinion. If a 401k works for you that's great. Everything is not for everybody.

Pensions are another way people can retire from their jobs. However many companies do not offer pensions. If they do, most likely there is a time limit on it. I remember when I was a kid hearing my Grandmother talk about her pension when she retired. Times have definitely changed.

Social Security is also a retirement option but it's not to be relied on especially by Millenials. Because people are living longer, social security isn't going to be sustainable with the amount of people retiring at one time. So what do people do now for retirement.

Well ask yourself this question. Am I saving for my retirement right now? If you are great! If not, you need to start. It's never to late to start, however you need to start. Whether you are saving or not you need to have a dollar amount in mind as a goal. If you make $50,000 a year, you need to have 20 times that to retire comfortably. Can you retire right now with one million dollars? Of course we can in 2018. But remember as time goes by you are going to need more than one million dollars. Why? Remember our friends taxes and inflation. They never go away and will always find a way to eat your money if you aren't careful.

So what is your ideal retirement

age?_______________________________________

____

How much money do you want to have coming in

monthly?___________________________

What is 20 times your annual

income?_____________________________________

____

Is the above number enough to retire

comfortably?________________________________

____

Are you on track for your

retirement?_________________________________

____

Are you saving for your retirement?________________________________

____

My retirement goal is to retire at 45 and travel the world. By this time my oldest child will be 18. By me saving for him as a child he will have his own money to do what he wants to do with his life and not have to tap into my retirement money. I have had many conversations with parents who are torn between sending their kids to college or retiring. I have had people tell me they have exhausted their 401k or other retirement plans just to send their kids to college. There are options to prevent this from happening. You can retire and your kids can go to college. You just have to know where to position your money. And you need to know how much money you need for both goals. Once you have the numbers. Discipline yourself to consistently save the amount that is needed. You got this!

Notes

Debt (It's not a bad thing)

What do you think of when you hear the word debt? For me it used to sound so ugly. But debt isn't actually a bad thing. Debt is placed into categories of good and bad, and installment or revolving. Yes debt can be good. There are two types of debt that are good. If you have them and you aren't paying or you defaulted you may see them as bad. However on your credit report (if you're in good standing) these debts are reported as good debts. So what is considered good debt? student loans and mortgages. I know it may be hard to believe. Especially considering that student loan debt surpasses mortgage and car loans.

Revolving credit is paying a balance to account not in full. Therefore balance carry off to the next month as well as interest. Installment payments are for student loan, mortgage and car loans. It's a debt that is paid off over time. So if you have $20,000 for a 5 year car loan with a 1.99% interest rate the monthly payment is $350. So that is the amount that you have to pay for the next five years to settle the debt.

Honestly to me doesn't matter what it is, debt is ok until it becomes unmanageable. Some people, especially young people(18-22) think that credit cards, student loans, car loans etc, are free money. So they open accounts and fail to repay them. The end result is multiple collections, garnishment of wages and a bad credit score. Once these things start happening, it's very difficult to fix. One of the reasons being is that little thing called interest. So remember when I talked about the rule of 72. It isn't just for positive investment. It works for debt too. If you have for example $100,000 of student loan debt at 15%, then your debt will double in 10 years. So if you make no payments at all $100,000 will become $200,000 in 10 years. Compound magic is a beautiful thing. Let it work for you not against you.

How much debt do you have in total?

Do you know the interest rate for each individual debt?

The only debt I have is student loan debt. It's a debt that I wish I didn't have for several reasons. One I went to school and have never used the degrees that I now have to pay for. It's crazy how we are encouraged to go to school but aren't guaranteed a job in our field of study. Matter of fact in some states you aren't even guaranteed a job. None of that even matters. The only thing that matters is that I am fully responsible for the $71,000 debt in my name. Word of advice, think very hard and long about your degree programs and school choices. It's not worth it to get in debt and not get a job to pay the debt. If you have massive debt, I encourage you to make an appointment with me for some debt management. It's free of charge. Why not have a professional look into some ways to help you reduce debt and liability. Get a handle on your debt before it gets a handle on you.

As part of our financial literacy campaign, we offer a series of eight free workshops. My office is located in the Bronx. Every week people come to learn more about personal finance. Our financial workshops consist of the following topics

1. Increase Cash Flow
2. Debt Management
3. Building a Strong Financial Foundation

4. Proper Protection
5. Building Wealth
6. Asset Accumulation
7. Retirement Planning
8. Wealth Preservation

I have seen all of these workshops multiple times. I have seen them so many times that I can now present them to families. The workshops are provided to give people basic personal finance education. So that you can get a handle on your own financial situation. Wouldn't you agree that if you keep doing the same things over and over, and they don't work, that it's time to try something new? Well the workshops, help you to see your personal finance in a new perspective.

If you don't live in NY, that is fine we still have workshops for you to see. Workshops are held all over the US and Canada. If you are interested in a specific state contact me and I will connect you to a financial center near you. If you can't get to the workshops, most provide online viewing options. My office does. So contact me to gain access to the live online session. When it comes to getting out of debt, we need to be serious and set some goals. It isn't going to work without discipline and consistency. Its the same way with losing weight. People make resolutions to go to the gym, eat healthy for the new year. They may keep their goals for 3 weeks to 3 months. And then what happens, they go back to the same habits. So can you commit to taking small steps to get out of debt? Your goals can be big but you can have smaller goals to get to the big goal.

Notes

Life Insurance (It's not death insurance)

Life insurance is a very debatable subject. People have their opinions on what is good or bad. Whats a scam or what to avoid. None of that matters though. The fact of the matter is that we all need life insurance. Don't think so, answer these questions.

1. What will happen when you die?
2. Who's paying for your funeral?

Will your family have the money to pay for your funeral or will they have to exhaust their savings, or create a go fund me. Life insurance is to protect us in the case of death. We all are going to die. We know this so why do we not protect our life. If you have kids, you should have life insurance. Of course that is not often the case. I have sat with a few families who don't have life insurance. Not having life insurance is done for many reasons. The most common reason is not being able to afford it. Another reason is not being educated. Single people with no kids are the ones who say they don't need life insurance. Well the same questions above apply. I actually asked someone this and she said "I didn't think about this"? No one wants to think about death but it's best to be prepared then unprepared when the time come.

Ask someone what type of life insurance they have and you'll hear one of two answers. Whole life or Term. Why is this when there are five types of life insurance policies a person can get. The answer is lack of financial education. I didn't know there were five types of insurance. I was in utter shock when I found this out. I'm going to run down the different types and explain how they work.

Life insurance comes in the form of being temporary or permanent. Temporary as we know means not forever, has an expiration date etc.... Term is the type of life of insurance that fits under the temporary umbrella. There is nothing wrong with having a term, however it is not a good fit for everyone. Before you buy any life insurance please do your due diligence and make sure it's the best for your family. Do not purchase because of the price or because someone said it's the best. In the long run you will pay for what you don't know. Term is just pure protection. You pay your premium and when you die your beneficiary. There is no cash value that will be accrued. You can get a term for five years, ten years, fifteen years, twenty years, twenty five or thirty years. The affordable price of the term is what attracts most people to it. However, most people just see or hear the price and sign up, overlooking the term conditions. Contracts exist for a reason. For consumers, it lets us know exactly what we are paying for. If you don't read or understand that is not the fault of the company. You need to make sure you understand and if you do not, do not give your money or sign the contract. I have a paralegal background. I see and hear this all the time. People don't read a contract and they say what they purchased was a scam. That the company tricked them. Upon taking a deeper look, the person didn't read and unfortunately there is nothing that can be done in most cases.

I keep hearing people say term is a scam or a waste of money. Again, everything is not for everybody. For some families a term makes sense. If you want to accrue a cash value, replace your income, etc then a term doesn't make sense for your family. Knowing that the term ends at a certain amount of years is what people should pay attention to. When the term expires you may be allowed to renew. That is up to the company and again will be outlined in the contract. If they let you renew you renew at the current age you are not the age you were. Does that make sense? Here's an example. If you purchased a twenty term at twenty and are paying $20, in twenty years you are forty. The price will now be at the rate of a forty year old. Which will most likely make $20 turn into $100+. Many people are aware of the renewable rates. They just see what they have to pay now. Ultimately you get what you pay for so choose carefully and wisely.

Under the permanent life insurance umbrella, there are four types. They are Whole life, Universal life, Index Universal life and Variable Universal life.

These policies all accrue cash value. They all work a little differently though. Even though they are all different, they serve the same purpose. To protect a family in the event of a loss.

Whole life is the oldest form of permanent insurance. It is also what most people know or have. It's interest rates are very conservative. It's a fixed product. So whatever your premium is that is the premium for the life of the policy. Whatever the due date is, you have to pay by that date or you risk your policy lapsing. As I said, whole life is what most people have and know. I highly suggest you sit with a financial professional like myself if you have a whole life policy. If you want to save for your kids college, your retirement, buy a house, then whole life cash accrual will not help you with your goal.

Universal life, Index Universal life, and Variable Universal life are all flexible policies. You have the ability to change the premium and skip payments. Index Universal life mirrors the Index. You can gain up to 15% depending on the company you choose. So your potential to grow your money is great. Because your money isn't directly in the stock market, you don't participate in the market losses. With the Variable life insurance policy you can gain and lose money. I wouldn't suggest this for people who are not stock market savvy. If you want more information about these three policy's feel free to reach out to me or your financial profession.

Most people think life insurance is death insurance. That is far beyond the truth. Life insurance has so many living benefits that can be used while alive. Long term care is one of them. Long

Now that you have learned a bit about the different types of life insurance I have some questions for you. If you can't answer the questions below then you need to sit down with a financial professional. Protecting your life is one of the most important steps to building a strong financial foundation.

What type of life insurance do you have?____________________________________

____

What company is your policy with?____________________________________

____

What is the amount of your death benefit?____________________________________

____

How much cash value have you accrued?____________________________________

____

The purpose of these questions are to get you thinking about your needs, goals and wants with life insurance. Most people purchase life insurance and have no clue what they have or anything about the policy. It's time to stop buying financial products with no knowledge of what you're paying for. If you don't have any life insurance do yourself a favor and reach out to me ASAP. Go Fund Me is not life insurance!!!!! Life insurance is so much more than a death benefit. Think about creating generational wealth for your children. Life insurance can do just that for your family. Think about it if you are gone who is taking care of your family? How will they be provided for with the loss of your income? These are the questions that need to be taken into consideration when purchasing life insurance. Life insurance is an investment. An investment that will have great benefits in the future.

Notes

Estate Planning (Not just for the rich and wealthy)

People don't like to talk about death. Death is inevitable. We work all our lives, gain assets and money, and some of us have no plans on what is to happen to our stuff when we die. After experiencing the death of my grandmother, I made sure to have my affairs in order. We hear too many times of celebrities not having wills or trusts. The most recent being the Queen of Soul, Aretha Franklin. Estate Planning is not just for rich people. Any one can get a will. The question is are you going to put in the work to get one done? Do you really want the government deciding who gets all of the stuff you worked so hard for?

Anything that you own is a part of your estate. You need to have a will to state who gets what in the event of your death. The will is a legal document stating your wishes for your property. The will names people that will care for your estate as well as establishes guardians for your minor children. This is very important. If you have minor children, you don't want to assume that someone will care for them. If you don't have a will, the court will decide where your children go. For me that is something, that I don't want to worry about. So I planned ahead. I have a will, living trust, and medical directives all signed and ready in the event of my passing.

There are many negative consequences to not having a will. Do you know or have you been apart of family arguments for stuff of someone who passed? Families tend to not get along during this time. Then there are people who don't have family and the government ends up taking control of the estate. So why not give yourself the peace of mind and have a will created. Again they aren't expensive and they don't take long to create. Estate planning is one of the workshops that I offer. If you need any assistance feel free to reach out to me.

This chapter is very short on purpose. Estate Planning is a legal matter which requires legal documents. I am not a lawyer. I am a paralegal but I can not give out legal advice. What I can do is connect you with legal services and attorneys who can assist you. In the meantime if you don't have a will, you need to ask your self these questions. These serves as a guide for who and what you will include in your will.

1. Are you married?________________________________

____

2. How many children do you have?___________________________________

____

3. Do you own a

home?______________________________________

____

____

4. How many assets do you

own?_______________________________________

____

____

5. Do you own any other real estate

property?____________________________________

____

____

6. Do you plan to have more

children?____________________________________

These questions will help you prepare a will. However know, that just because you have a will that doesn't mean that it can't or won't be contested in court. Just having the document protects you more than not having it at all. A will can be revised at anytime if it is revocable. The choice is your in deciding which type of will to give. Consult an attorney for all of your estate planning needs. Need an attorney contact me and I can get you connected.

Notes

Mindset and Goals (important for decisions to be made)

The one simple thing in life that we can do is what most people won't do. Change their mindset. Mindset is part of the reason why people stay stuck in the same old situations that they are tired of. Have you ever heard someone say they want to start their own business? That they are sick and tired of working for someone else? Yet they won't take the leap to get started in their business. And continue to go to the very job that they hate. I'm sure some people spend time crying and dreading going to work. To convince themselves to stay they say thing like the pay is good or the benefits are great. Why be miserable just to have someone else reap the benefit. Yes you get paid to work but not what you want or know that you are worth. A change of mindset would let them know that they can change their reality. People have to decide to change not want to change. Wanting to change can be a thought with no type of action. Deciding to change means a person has come up with a game plan to go after their dreams and do whatever it takes. Once the shift of mindset starts, (it's a process that's lifelong) you will have to do things you never imagined doing. Your friends and family will be concerned, negative or leave you alone while you undergo transformation. You'll have to believe in things that you can't see yet. Push past your fears, fail (they say failure is not an option but it is required to be successful) and do some uncomfortable things. Let go of things that are old and limit you to become the person that you desire to be. Does this sound challenging? Of course, it is!!! But this challenge is nowhere as miserable as the challenge you face today. You don't want to have a breakthrough when your life is in chaos. Hitting rock bottom shouldn't force people to start making changes. The decision to change should be made before you hit the bottom. All it takes is one decision. So if you have a dream or goal, you have two options. Accept the fact that people close to you most likely won't support and keep it moving, or sulk and give up on your dream and help others with their dreams.

The same concept goes for your finances. Once you make the decision to do better and improve your financial situation, all hell is going to break loose. You are going to hear things such as “You think you are better than us”, “You can’t do it” etc. I know cause I heard this plus more. I had people questioning me when I said I wanted to purchase a home in two years. When you make a decision to embark on a financial change, you need to be secure in the decision. You need to have the faith and belief that you can do it. Otherwise people will get in your head and deter you from making any changes. Me personally I refuse to be broke. I know what that felt like as a child. I do not want to ever tell my children no they can't have one of their basic needs meet.

The financial journey of change is going to be challenging. There is going to be a lot of things you don't know. However as consumers,we have a responsibility to ourselves to do our due diligence. If we are unsure then we need to dig a little deeper or hold off on whatever it is you want at the moment.

So I know you have goals. We all do. I want to buy a home on both the east and west coast. I want to be a motivational speaker. I want to travel the world. When we make goals we have to be specific and put a time on them. If we don't then they are just dreams that may or may not happen. Your goals can be as big as you want. I suggest breaking them into smaller goals so you won't be overwhelmed. Being overwhelmed stops most people from accomplishing what they want to do

1. What are your short goals?____________________________________

____

2. What are your long term goals?____________________________________

____

3. Are your goals specific?____________________________________

____

4. Are your goals realistic?____________________________________

____

I hope that you have taken something from this book to apply it your situation. I wish you the best of luck on your financial journey! If you have any questions feel free to reach out to me. Welcome to being the best version of you!

Notes

Made in the USA
Monee, IL
04 November 2026

67379784R00056